INTERNET PASSWORD LOGBOOK
*Never again spend frantic minutes searching
for scraps of paper containing website
addresses, usernames, logins, or passwords.
Note them in this handy book!*

**ROCK
POINT**

NEW YORK, NEW YORK

First published in 2014 by RockPoint, an imprint of
Quarto Publishing Group USA Inc., 276 Fifth Ave, Suite 206,
New York, NY 10001

This title is also available at discounts in bulk quantity for industrial
or sales-promotional use. For details write to Special Sales Manager
at Quarto Publishing Group USA Inc., 276 Fifth Ave, Suite 206,
New York, NY 10001

Library of Congress Cataloging-in-Publication Data

ISBN: 978-1-59186-908-5

Acquisitions Editor: Billie Brownell
Book Interior Art Director: Cindy Samargia Laun

Cover Pattern Design: Jane Dixon
Cover Design: Heidi North

Printed in China
10 9 8 7 6 5 4 3 2 1

INTRODUCTION
Stop! *Please read the following.*

The purpose of our *Internet Password Logbook* is to make your life easier by providing a way to organize and record the endless and ever-changing usernames, passwords, special notes, and the myriad website addresses that are an integral part of your life.

Please take a moment to read the following section regarding tips on Internet safety and how to construct usernames and passwords that will be secure. This book is then organized into alpha sections to record this data, followed by locations to record software license information, home network settings, additional/overflow passwords, and a notes section.

Important Note: *the publisher of this book cannot be held responsible or liable for any damages, errors, consequences, or losses that may result from any user recording and storing data in this book.*

This is extremely sensitive information. Keep it in a safe and secure location, preferably one that only you know. The publisher recommends that you do not travel with this book. It is as valuable as a passport, and should be treated as carefully.

INTERNET PASSWORD SAFETY AND NAMING TIPS

It's very tempting to create login names and passwords that are easy to remember. Some people even use the same password for multiple accounts. But that's just not a good idea, and neither is using a recognizable word for passwords. In the digital age, that's just asking for trouble. Hackers have developed password-cracking software that can endlessly run thousands of options—until they find the right combination. The weaker your password—using real words or names associated with your accounts (especially anything posted to social media sites), reusing passwords, creating short logins or password names, for example— the more likely it is for hackers to crack your code.

You can make your accounts more secure by following the **How to Create Hacker-Proof Logins and Passwords** tips, recommended by security experts, to create secure passwords.

Secure passwords alone are not enough to protect you. Follow the tips in **Keeping Logins and Passwords Safe** to further protect your online identities.

HOW TO CREATE HACKER-PROOF
LOGINS AND PASSWORDS

Tips for making your logins and passwords hacker-proof:

- The longer the name, the harder it is to crack. Experts recommend that logins and/or passwords be *at least* 8 characters in length (some sites have a minimum number of required characters, but even if the required number is fewer, aim for more than the minimum number of characters when allowed). The longer your password, the longer it will take a person or a program to crack it.
- Use a combination of uppercase and lowercase letters, characters, numbers, and symbols. Avoid using all letters or all numbers.
- Use a random approach (literally random) or a system that only you would know, such as substituting symbols for letters.
- Absolutely do *not* use Social Security numbers or phone numbers. Day/month combinations (such as birthdays) are considered vulnerable. So are things that are "known" about you, such as a license plate number, or your date of graduation or marriage.
- Don't use proper names—this means you, your spouse, your kids, your pets.
- Do not use any word that can be found in the dictionary (not even foreign words or phrases).
- Do not use the same word in your password as your login; make them as wildly different as possible.
- Avoid "logical" combinations, such as "ABC" or "123" in the string.
- Change your logins and passwords—often.
- Avoid re-using a login or password for a year—or never.
- If the site analyzes the "strength" of your password, make sure your password meets the strongest indication.

Here are a couple of examples:

- **Select a word, spell it backwards, and insert numbers and/or symbols in it.** For example, "street" spelled backwards is "teerts"—you could incorporate your street name and address. (Don't do this if your address actually includes the word "street," use another word.) Let's say you use the first two letters of the word spelled backwards, then the first number of your address, then two letters of your actual street address. Then repeat (but avoid spelling an actual word). So, for an example, if your address is 410 River Road, try "te4Rier1vets0rR"—just end it to avoid including an actual word. (But write it down in this book!) There are also websites that create randomly generated combinations.

- **Use mnemonic devices.** For example, think of a phrase (maybe it's a song title, maybe it's a line from a book), and use the first letter from each word. Throw in some uppercase letters, numbers, and symbols for good measure. Here's an example: "It was the best of times, it was the worst of times" = "iwtbotiwtwot." You're not done. *A Tale of Two Cities*, by Charles Dickens, from which this quote came, was written in 1859. So maybe it becomes, "iwtC9bot5iwtD8wot1#"—and there you have a 19-character login or password.

Some experts say it's
not *if*, it's *when* your
security will be breached.

KEEPING LOGINS AND PASSWORDS SAFE

Once you've created some hard-to-crack passwords, another step is to safeguard your passwords and logins (beyond changing them frequently). Some tips to remember include:

- Do not log into secure sites at unsecure Wi-Fi locations (the airport, coffee shops, and Internet cafes, for example).
- Never email your login or password to another person.
- Do not tell *anyone* your logins or passwords, not even your best friend. They may not always be your friend.
- Keep this *Internet Password Logbook* in a secure location that only you know; it's as valuable as your passport.
- Change your login or password often (that one is noted in this article twice for a reason).
- Take advantage if a site offers a series of password hint security questions; some even let you write the question. But, don't answer it logically; use a response that only you would know. If the site's security question is "Your mother's maiden name" then set the "answer" to be a favorite song title.
- Maintain an overall Internet security system to guard against malware.
- Use a different login/password for every account.
- Be cautious about the amount and type of information you put on social media; all of it can be used by hackers to gain information about you.

Remember to be diligent with your online accounts. Cyber criminals are everywhere and by following the tips in the *Internet Password Logbook*, you can make it harder for cyber criminals to gain access to your online accounts and passwords.

Use a combination of letters, numbers, and symbols.

The longer your logins and passwords, the harder they are to crack.

Do not tell anyone your logins or passwords, not even your best friend.

Don't use any word that's in the dictionary.

Change your logins and passwords often.

WEBSITE

Username:

Date/Password:

Date/Password:

Date/Password:

Date/Password:

Date/Password:

WEBSITE

Username:

Date/Password:

Date/Password:

Date/Password:

Date/Password:

Date/Password:

WEBSITE

Username:

Date/Password:

Date/Password:

Date/Password:

Date/Password:

Date/Password:

WEBSITE

Username:

Date/Password:

Date/Password:

Date/Password:

Date/Password:

Date/Password:

WEBSITE

Username:

Date/Password:

Date/Password:

Date/Password:

Date/Password:

Date/Password:

WEBSITE

Username:

Date/Password:

Date/Password:

Date/Password:

Date/Password:

Date/Password:

WEBSITE

Username:

Date/Password:

Date/Password:

Date/Password:

Date/Password:

Date/Password:

WEBSITE

Username:

Date/Password:

Date/Password:

Date/Password:

Date/Password:

Date/Password:

WEBSITE

Username:

Date/Password:

Date/Password:

Date/Password:

Date/Password:

Date/Password:

WEBSITE

Username:

Date/Password:

Date/Password:

Date/Password:

Date/Password:

Date/Password:

WEBSITE

Username:

Date/Password:

Date/Password:

Date/Password:

Date/Password:

Date/Password:

WEBSITE

Username:

Date/Password:

Date/Password:

Date/Password:

Date/Password:

Date/Password:

WEBSITE

Username:

Date/Password:

Date/Password:

Date/Password:

Date/Password:

Date/Password:

WEBSITE

Username:

Date/Password:

Date/Password:

Date/Password:

Date/Password:

Date/Password:

WEBSITE

Username:

Date/Password:

Date/Password:

Date/Password:

Date/Password:

Date/Password:

WEBSITE

Username:

Date/Password:

Date/Password:

Date/Password:

Date/Password:

Date/Password:

WEBSITE

Username:

Date/Password:

Date/Password:

Date/Password:

Date/Password:

Date/Password:

WEBSITE

Username:

Date/Password:

Date/Password:

Date/Password:

Date/Password:

Date/Password:

WEBSITE

Username:

Date/Password:

Date/Password:

Date/Password:

Date/Password:

Date/Password:

WEBSITE

Username:

Date/Password:

Date/Password:

Date/Password:

Date/Password:

Date/Password:

WEBSITE

Username:

Date/Password:

Date/Password:

Date/Password:

Date/Password:

Date/Password:

WEBSITE

Username:

Date/Password:

Date/Password:

Date/Password:

Date/Password:

Date/Password: .

WEBSITE

Username:

Date/Password:

Date/Password:

Date/Password:

Date/Password:

Date/Password:

WEBSITE

Username:

Date/Password:

Date/Password:

Date/Password:

Date/Password:

Date/Password:

WEBSITE

Username:

Date/Password:

Date/Password:

Date/Password:

Date/Password:

Date/Password:

WEBSITE

Username:

Date/Password:

Date/Password:

Date/Password:

Date/Password:

Date/Password:

WEBSITE

Username:

Date/Password:

Date/Password:

Date/Password:

Date/Password:

Date/Password:

WEBSITE

Username:

Date/Password:

Date/Password:

Date/Password:

Date/Password:

Date/Password:

WEBSITE

Username:

Date/Password:

Date/Password:

Date/Password:

Date/Password:

Date/Password:

WEBSITE

Username:

Date/Password:

Date/Password:

Date/Password:

Date/Password:

Date/Password:

WEBSITE

Username:

Date/Password:

Date/Password:

Date/Password:

Date/Password:

Date/Password:

WEBSITE

Username:

Date/Password:

Date/Password:

Date/Password:

Date/Password:

Date/Password:

WEBSITE

Username:

Date/Password:

Date/Password:

Date/Password:

Date/Password:

Date/Password:

WEBSITE

Username:

Date/Password:

Date/Password:

Date/Password:

Date/Password:

Date/Password:

WEBSITE

Username:

Date/Password:

Date/Password:

Date/Password:

Date/Password:

Date/Password:

WEBSITE

Username:

Date/Password:

Date/Password:

Date/Password:

Date/Password:

Date/Password:

WEBSITE

Username:

Date/Password:

Date/Password:

Date/Password:

Date/Password:

Date/Password:

WEBSITE

Username:

Date/Password:

Date/Password:

Date/Password:

Date/Password:

Date/Password:

WEBSITE

Username:

Date/Password:

Date/Password:

Date/Password:

Date/Password:

Date/Password:

WEBSITE

Username:

Date/Password:

Date/Password:

Date/Password:

Date/Password:

Date/Password:

WEBSITE

Username:

Date/Password:

Date/Password:

Date/Password:

Date/Password:

Date/Password:

WEBSITE

Username:

Date/Password:

Date/Password:

Date/Password:

Date/Password:

Date/Password:

WEBSITE

Username:

Date/Password:

Date/Password:

Date/Password:

Date/Password:

Date/Password:

WEBSITE

Username:

Date/Password:

Date/Password:

Date/Password:

Date/Password:

Date/Password:

WEBSITE

Username:

Date/Password:

Date/Password:

Date/Password:

Date/Password:

Date/Password:

WEBSITE

Username:

Date/Password:

Date/Password:

Date/Password:

Date/Password:

Date/Password:

WEBSITE

Username:

Date/Password:

Date/Password:

Date/Password:

Date/Password:

Date/Password:

WEBSITE

Username:

Date/Password:

Date/Password:

Date/Password:

Date/Password:

Date/Password:

WEBSITE

Username:

Date/Password:

Date/Password:

Date/Password:

Date/Password:

Date/Password:

WEBSITE

Username:

Date/Password:

Date/Password:

Date/Password:

Date/Password:

Date/Password:

WEBSITE

Username:

Date/Password:

Date/Password:

Date/Password:

Date/Password:

Date/Password:

WEBSITE

Username:

Date/Password:

Date/Password:

Date/Password:

Date/Password:

Date/Password:

WEBSITE

Username:

Date/Password:

Date/Password:

Date/Password:

Date/Password:

Date/Password:

WEBSITE

Username:

Date/Password:

Date/Password:

Date/Password:

Date/Password:

Date/Password:

WEBSITE

Username:

Date/Password:

Date/Password:

Date/Password:

Date/Password:

Date/Password:

WEBSITE

Username:

Date/Password:

Date/Password:

Date/Password:

Date/Password:

Date/Password:

WEBSITE

Username:

Date/Password:

Date/Password:

Date/Password:

Date/Password:

Date/Password:

WEBSITE

Username:

Date/Password:

Date/Password:

Date/Password:

Date/Password:

Date/Password:

WEBSITE

Username:

Date/Password:

Date/Password:

Date/Password:

Date/Password:

Date/Password:

WEBSITE

Username:

Date/Password:

Date/Password:

Date/Password:

Date/Password:

Date/Password:

WEBSITE

Username:

Date/Password:

Date/Password:

Date/Password:

Date/Password:

Date/Password:

WEBSITE

Username:

Date/Password:

Date/Password:

Date/Password:

Date/Password:

Date/Password:

WEBSITE

Username:

Date/Password:

Date/Password:

Date/Password:

Date/Password:

Date/Password:

WEBSITE

Username:

Date/Password:

Date/Password:

Date/Password:

Date/Password:

Date/Password:

WEBSITE

Username:

Date/Password:

Date/Password:

Date/Password:

Date/Password:

Date/Password:

WEBSITE

Username:

Date/Password:

Date/Password:

Date/Password:

Date/Password:

Date/Password:

WEBSITE

Username:

Date/Password:

Date/Password:

Date/Password:

Date/Password:

Date/Password:

WEBSITE

Username:

Date/Password:

Date/Password:

Date/Password:

Date/Password:

Date/Password:

WEBSITE

Username:

Date/Password:

Date/Password:

Date/Password:

Date/Password:

Date/Password:

WEBSITE

Username:

Date/Password:

Date/Password:

Date/Password:

Date/Password:

Date/Password:

WEBSITE

Username:

Date/Password:

Date/Password:

Date/Password:

Date/Password:

Date/Password:

WEBSITE

Username:

Date/Password:

Date/Password:

Date/Password:

Date/Password:

Date/Password:

WEBSITE

Username:

Date/Password:

Date/Password:

Date/Password:

Date/Password:

Date/Password:

WEBSITE

Username:

Date/Password:

Date/Password:

Date/Password:

Date/Password:

Date/Password:

WEBSITE

Username:

Date/Password:

Date/Password:

Date/Password:

Date/Password:

Date/Password:

WEBSITE

Username:

Date/Password:

Date/Password:

Date/Password:

Date/Password:

Date/Password:

WEBSITE

Username:

Date/Password:

Date/Password:

Date/Password:

Date/Password:

Date/Password:

WEBSITE

Username:

Date/Password:

Date/Password:

Date/Password:

Date/Password:

Date/Password:

WEBSITE

Username:

Date/Password:

Date/Password:

Date/Password:

Date/Password:

Date/Password:

WEBSITE

Username:

Date/Password:

Date/Password:

Date/Password:

Date/Password:

Date/Password:

WEBSITE

Username:

Date/Password:

Date/Password:

Date/Password:

Date/Password:

Date/Password:

WEBSITE

Username:

Date/Password:

Date/Password:

Date/Password:

Date/Password:

Date/Password:

WEBSITE

Username:

Date/Password:

Date/Password:

Date/Password:

Date/Password:

Date/Password:

WEBSITE

Username:

Date/Password:

Date/Password:

Date/Password:

Date/Password:

Date/Password:

WEBSITE

Username:

Date/Password:

Date/Password:

Date/Password:

Date/Password:

Date/Password:

WEBSITE

Username:

Date/Password:

Date/Password:

Date/Password:

Date/Password:

Date/Password:

WEBSITE

Username:

Date/Password:

Date/Password:

Date/Password:

Date/Password:

Date/Password:

WEBSITE

Username:

Date/Password:

Date/Password:

Date/Password:

Date/Password:

Date/Password:

WEBSITE

Username:

Date/Password:

Date/Password:

Date/Password:

Date/Password:

Date/Password:

WEBSITE

Username:

Date/Password:

Date/Password:

Date/Password:

Date/Password:

Date/Password:

WEBSITE

Username:

Date/Password:

Date/Password:

Date/Password:

Date/Password:

Date/Password:

WEBSITE

Username:

Date/Password:

Date/Password:

Date/Password:

Date/Password:

Date/Password:

WEBSITE

Username:

Date/Password:

Date/Password:

Date/Password:

Date/Password:

Date/Password:

WEBSITE

Username:

Date/Password:

Date/Password:

Date/Password:

Date/Password:

Date/Password:

WEBSITE

Username:

Date/Password:

Date/Password:

Date/Password:

Date/Password:

Date/Password:

WEBSITE

Username:

Date/Password:

Date/Password:

Date/Password:

Date/Password:

Date/Password:

WEBSITE

Username:

Date/Password:

Date/Password:

Date/Password:

Date/Password:

Date/Password:

WEBSITE

Username:

Date/Password:

Date/Password:

Date/Password:

Date/Password:

Date/Password:

WEBSITE

Username:

Date/Password:

Date/Password:

Date/Password:

Date/Password:

Date/Password:

WEBSITE

Username:

Date/Password:

Date/Password:

Date/Password:

Date/Password:

Date/Password:

WEBSITE

Username:

Date/Password:

Date/Password:

Date/Password:

Date/Password:

Date/Password:

WEBSITE

Username:

Date/Password:

Date/Password:

Date/Password:

Date/Password:

Date/Password:

WEBSITE

Username:

Date/Password:

Date/Password:

Date/Password:

Date/Password:

Date/Password:

WEBSITE

Username:

Date/Password:

Date/Password:

Date/Password:

Date/Password:

Date/Password:

WEBSITE

Username:

Date/Password:

Date/Password:

Date/Password:

Date/Password:

Date/Password:

WEBSITE

Username:

Date/Password:

Date/Password:

Date/Password:

Date/Password:

Date/Password:

WEBSITE

Username:

Date/Password:

Date/Password:

Date/Password:

Date/Password:

Date/Password:

WEBSITE

Username:

Date/Password:

Date/Password:

Date/Password:

Date/Password:

Date/Password:

WEBSITE

Username:

Date/Password:

Date/Password:

Date/Password:

Date/Password:

Date/Password:

WEBSITE

Username:

Date/Password:

Date/Password:

Date/Password:

Date/Password:

Date/Password:

WEBSITE

Username:

Date/Password:

Date/Password:

Date/Password:

Date/Password:

Date/Password:

WEBSITE

Username:

Date/Password:

Date/Password:

Date/Password:

Date/Password:

Date/Password:

WEBSITE

Username:

Date/Password:

Date/Password:

Date/Password:

Date/Password:

Date/Password:

WEBSITE

Username:

Date/Password:

Date/Password:

Date/Password:

Date/Password:

Date/Password:

WEBSITE

Username:

Date/Password:

Date/Password:

Date/Password:

Date/Password:

Date/Password:

WEBSITE

Username:

Date/Password:

Date/Password:

Date/Password:

Date/Password:

Date/Password:

WEBSITE

Username:

Date/Password:

Date/Password:

Date/Password:

Date/Password:

Date/Password:

WEBSITE

Username:

Date/Password:

Date/Password:

Date/Password:

Date/Password:

Date/Password:

WEBSITE

Username:

Date/Password:

Date/Password:

Date/Password:

Date/Password:

Date/Password:

WEBSITE

Username:

Date/Password:

Date/Password:

Date/Password:

Date/Password:

Date/Password:

WEBSITE

Username:

Date/Password:

Date/Password:

Date/Password:

Date/Password:

Date/Password:

WEBSITE

Username:

Date/Password:

Date/Password:

Date/Password:

Date/Password:

Date/Password:

WEBSITE

Username:

Date/Password:

Date/Password:

Date/Password:

Date/Password:

Date/Password:

K
L

WEBSITE

Username:

Date/Password:

Date/Password:

Date/Password:

Date/Password:

Date/Password:

WEBSITE

Username:

Date/Password:

Date/Password:

Date/Password:

Date/Password:

Date/Password:

WEBSITE

Username:

Date/Password:

Date/Password:

Date/Password:

Date/Password:

Date/Password:

WEBSITE

Username:

Date/Password:

Date/Password:

Date/Password:

Date/Password:

Date/Password:

WEBSITE

Username:

Date/Password:

Date/Password:

Date/Password:

Date/Password:

Date/Password:

WEBSITE

Username:

Date/Password:

Date/Password:

Date/Password:

Date/Password:

Date/Password:

K
L

WEBSITE

Username:

Date/Password:

Date/Password:

Date/Password:

Date/Password:

Date/Password:

WEBSITE

Username:

Date/Password:

Date/Password:

Date/Password:

Date/Password:

Date/Password:

WEBSITE

Username:

Date/Password:

Date/Password:

Date/Password:

Date/Password:

Date/Password:

WEBSITE

Username:

Date/Password:

Date/Password:

Date/Password:

Date/Password:

Date/Password:

WEBSITE

Username:

Date/Password:

Date/Password:

Date/Password:

Date/Password:

Date/Password:

WEBSITE

Username:

Date/Password:

Date/Password:

Date/Password:

Date/Password:

Date/Password:

K
L

K
L

WEBSITE

Username:

Date/Password:

Date/Password:

Date/Password:

Date/Password:

Date/Password:

WEBSITE

Username:

Date/Password:

Date/Password:

Date/Password:

Date/Password:

Date/Password:

WEBSITE

Username:

Date/Password:

Date/Password:

Date/Password:

Date/Password:

Date/Password:

WEBSITE

Username:

Date/Password:

Date/Password:

Date/Password:

Date/Password:

Date/Password:

WEBSITE

Username:

Date/Password:

Date/Password:

Date/Password:

Date/Password:

Date/Password:

WEBSITE

Username:

Date/Password:

Date/Password:

Date/Password:

Date/Password:

Date/Password:

K
L

WEBSITE

Username:

Date/Password:

Date/Password:

Date/Password:

Date/Password:

Date/Password:

WEBSITE

Username:

Date/Password:

Date/Password:

Date/Password:

Date/Password:

Date/Password:

WEBSITE

Username:

Date/Password:

Date/Password:

Date/Password:

Date/Password:

Date/Password:

WEBSITE

Username:

Date/Password:

Date/Password:

Date/Password:

Date/Password:

Date/Password:

WEBSITE

Username:

Date/Password:

Date/Password:

Date/Password:

Date/Password:

Date/Password:

WEBSITE

Username:

Date/Password:

Date/Password:

Date/Password:

Date/Password:

Date/Password:

WEBSITE

Username:

Date/Password:

Date/Password:

Date/Password:

Date/Password:

Date/Password:

WEBSITE

Username:

Date/Password:

Date/Password:

Date/Password:

Date/Password:

Date/Password:

WEBSITE

Username:

Date/Password:

Date/Password:

Date/Password:

Date/Password:

Date/Password:

WEBSITE

Username:

Date/Password:

Date/Password:

Date/Password:

Date/Password:

Date/Password:

WEBSITE

Username:

Date/Password:

Date/Password:

Date/Password:

Date/Password:

Date/Password:

WEBSITE

Username:

Date/Password:

Date/Password:

Date/Password:

Date/Password:

Date/Password:

WEBSITE

Username:

Date/Password:

Date/Password:

Date/Password:

Date/Password:

Date/Password:

WEBSITE

Username:

Date/Password:

Date/Password:

Date/Password:

Date/Password:

Date/Password:

WEBSITE

Username:

Date/Password:

Date/Password:

Date/Password:

Date/Password:

Date/Password:

WEBSITE

Username:

Date/Password:

Date/Password:

Date/Password:

Date/Password:

Date/Password:

WEBSITE

Username:

Date/Password:

Date/Password:

Date/Password:

Date/Password:

Date/Password:

WEBSITE

Username:

Date/Password:

Date/Password:

Date/Password:

Date/Password:

Date/Password:

WEBSITE

Username:

Date/Password:

Date/Password:

Date/Password:

Date/Password:

Date/Password:

WEBSITE

Username:

Date/Password:

Date/Password:

Date/Password:

Date/Password:

Date/Password:

WEBSITE

Username:

Date/Password:

Date/Password:

Date/Password:

Date/Password:

Date/Password:

WEBSITE

Username:

Date/Password:

Date/Password:

Date/Password:

Date/Password:

Date/Password:

WEBSITE

Username:

Date/Password:

Date/Password:

Date/Password:

Date/Password:

Date/Password:

WEBSITE

Username:

Date/Password:

Date/Password:

Date/Password:

Date/Password:

Date/Password:

WEBSITE

Username:

Date/Password:

Date/Password:

Date/Password:

Date/Password:

Date/Password:

WEBSITE

Username:

Date/Password:

Date/Password:

Date/Password:

Date/Password:

Date/Password:

WEBSITE

Username:

Date/Password:

Date/Password:

Date/Password:

Date/Password:

Date/Password:

WEBSITE

Username:

Date/Password:

Date/Password:

Date/Password:

Date/Password:

Date/Password:

WEBSITE

Username:

Date/Password:

Date/Password:

Date/Password:

Date/Password:

Date/Password:

WEBSITE

Username:

Date/Password:

Date/Password:

Date/Password:

Date/Password:

Date/Password:

WEBSITE

Username:

Date/Password:

Date/Password:

Date/Password:

Date/Password:

Date/Password:

WEBSITE

Username:

Date/Password:

Date/Password:

Date/Password:

Date/Password:

Date/Password:

WEBSITE

Username:

Date/Password:

Date/Password:

Date/Password:

Date/Password:

Date/Password:

WEBSITE

Username:

Date/Password:

Date/Password:

Date/Password:

Date/Password:

Date/Password:

WEBSITE

Username:

Date/Password:

Date/Password:

Date/Password:

Date/Password:

Date/Password:

WEBSITE

Username:

Date/Password:

Date/Password:

Date/Password:

Date/Password:

Date/Password:

WEBSITE

Username:

Date/Password:

Date/Password:

Date/Password:

Date/Password:

Date/Password:

WEBSITE

Username:

Date/Password:

Date/Password:

Date/Password:

Date/Password:

Date/Password:

WEBSITE

Username:

Date/Password:

Date/Password:

Date/Password:

Date/Password:

Date/Password:

WEBSITE

Username:

Date/Password:

Date/Password:

Date/Password:

Date/Password:

Date/Password:

WEBSITE

Username:

Date/Password:

Date/Password:

Date/Password:

Date/Password:

Date/Password:

WEBSITE

Username:

Date/Password:

Date/Password:

Date/Password:

Date/Password:

Date/Password:

O
P

WEBSITE

Username:

Date/Password:

Date/Password:

Date/Password:

Date/Password:

Date/Password:

WEBSITE

Username:

Date/Password:

Date/Password:

Date/Password:

Date/Password:

Date/Password:

WEBSITE

Username:

Date/Password:

Date/Password:

Date/Password:

Date/Password:

Date/Password:

WEBSITE

Username:

Date/Password:

Date/Password:

Date/Password:

Date/Password:

Date/Password:

WEBSITE

Username:

Date/Password:

Date/Password:

Date/Password:

Date/Password:

Date/Password:

WEBSITE

Username:

Date/Password:

Date/Password:

Date/Password:

Date/Password:

Date/Password:

WEBSITE

Username:

Date/Password:

Date/Password:

Date/Password:

Date/Password:

Date/Password:

WEBSITE

Username:

Date/Password:

Date/Password:

Date/Password:

Date/Password:

Date/Password:

WEBSITE

Username:

Date/Password:

Date/Password:

Date/Password:

Date/Password:

Date/Password:

WEBSITE

Username:

Date/Password:

Date/Password:

Date/Password:

Date/Password:

Date/Password:

WEBSITE

Username:

Date/Password:

Date/Password:

Date/Password:

Date/Password:

Date/Password:

Q
R

WEBSITE

Username:

Date/Password:

Date/Password:

Date/Password:

Date/Password:

Date/Password:

WEBSITE

Username:

Date/Password:

Date/Password:

Date/Password:

Date/Password:

Date/Password:

WEBSITE

Username:

Date/Password:

Date/Password:

Date/Password:

Date/Password:

Date/Password:

WEBSITE

Username:

Date/Password:

Date/Password:

Date/Password:

Date/Password:

Date/Password:

WEBSITE

Username:

Date/Password:

Date/Password:

Date/Password:

Date/Password:

Date/Password:

WEBSITE

Username:

Date/Password:

Date/Password:

Date/Password:

Date/Password:

Date/Password:

WEBSITE

Username:

Date/Password:

Date/Password:

Date/Password:

Date/Password:

Date/Password:

WEBSITE

Username:

Date/Password:

Date/Password:

Date/Password:

Date/Password:

Date/Password:

WEBSITE

Username:

Date/Password:

Date/Password:

Date/Password:

Date/Password:

Date/Password:

WEBSITE

Username:

Date/Password:

Date/Password:

Date/Password:

Date/Password:

Date/Password:

WEBSITE

Username:

Date/Password:

Date/Password:

Date/Password:

Date/Password:

Date/Password:

WEBSITE

Username:

Date/Password:

Date/Password:

Date/Password:

Date/Password:

Date/Password:

WEBSITE

Username:

Date/Password:

Date/Password:

Date/Password:

Date/Password:

Date/Password:

Q
R

WEBSITE

Username:

Date/Password:

Date/Password:

Date/Password:

Date/Password:

Date/Password:

WEBSITE

Username:

Date/Password:

Date/Password:

Date/Password:

Date/Password:

Date/Password:

WEBSITE

Username:

Date/Password:

Date/Password:

Date/Password:

Date/Password:

Date/Password:

WEBSITE

Username:

Date/Password:

Date/Password:

Date/Password:

Date/Password:

Date/Password:

WEBSITE

Username:

Date/Password:

Date/Password:

Date/Password:

Date/Password:

Date/Password:

WEBSITE

Username:

Date/Password:

Date/Password:

Date/Password:

Date/Password:

Date/Password:

Q
R

WEBSITE

Username:

Date/Password:

Date/Password:

Date/Password:

Date/Password:

Date/Password:

WEBSITE

Username:

Date/Password:

Date/Password:

Date/Password:

Date/Password:

Date/Password:

WEBSITE

Username:

Date/Password:

Date/Password:

Date/Password:

Date/Password:

Date/Password:

WEBSITE

Username:

Date/Password:

Date/Password:

Date/Password:

Date/Password:

Date/Password:

WEBSITE

Username:

Date/Password:

Date/Password:

Date/Password:

Date/Password:

Date/Password:

WEBSITE

Username:

Date/Password:

Date/Password:

Date/Password:

Date/Password:

Date/Password:

WEBSITE

Username:

Date/Password:

Date/Password:

Date/Password:

Date/Password:

Date/Password:

WEBSITE

Username:

Date/Password:

Date/Password:

Date/Password:

Date/Password:

Date/Password:

WEBSITE

Username:

Date/Password:

Date/Password:

Date/Password:

Date/Password:

Date/Password:

WEBSITE

Username:

Date/Password:

Date/Password:

Date/Password:

Date/Password:

Date/Password:

WEBSITE

Username:

Date/Password:

Date/Password:

Date/Password:

Date/Password:

Date/Password:

WEBSITE

Username:

Date/Password:

Date/Password:

Date/Password:

Date/Password:

Date/Password:

S
T

WEBSITE

Username:

Date/Password:

Date/Password:

Date/Password:

Date/Password:

Date/Password:

WEBSITE

Username:

Date/Password:

Date/Password:

Date/Password:

Date/Password:

Date/Password:

WEBSITE

Username:

Date/Password:

Date/Password:

Date/Password:

Date/Password:

Date/Password:

WEBSITE

Username:

Date/Password:

Date/Password:

Date/Password:

Date/Password:

Date/Password:

WEBSITE

Username:

Date/Password:

Date/Password:

Date/Password:

Date/Password:

Date/Password:

WEBSITE

Username:

Date/Password:

Date/Password:

Date/Password:

Date/Password:

Date/Password:

S
T

WEBSITE

Username:

Date/Password:

Date/Password:

Date/Password:

Date/Password:

Date/Password:

WEBSITE

Username:

Date/Password:

Date/Password:

Date/Password:

Date/Password:

Date/Password:

WEBSITE

Username:

Date/Password:

Date/Password:

Date/Password:

Date/Password:

Date/Password:

WEBSITE

Username:

Date/Password:

Date/Password:

Date/Password:

Date/Password:

Date/Password:

WEBSITE

Username:

Date/Password:

Date/Password:

Date/Password:

Date/Password:

Date/Password:

WEBSITE

Username:

Date/Password:

Date/Password:

Date/Password:

Date/Password:

Date/Password:

WEBSITE

Username:

Date/Password:

Date/Password:

Date/Password:

Date/Password:

Date/Password:

WEBSITE

Username:

Date/Password:

Date/Password:

Date/Password:

Date/Password:

Date/Password:

WEBSITE

Username:

Date/Password:

Date/Password:

Date/Password:

Date/Password:

Date/Password:

WEBSITE

Username:

Date/Password:

Date/Password:

Date/Password:

Date/Password:

Date/Password:

WEBSITE

Username:

Date/Password:

Date/Password:

Date/Password:

Date/Password:

Date/Password:

WEBSITE

Username:

Date/Password:

Date/Password:

Date/Password:

Date/Password:

Date/Password:

U
V

WEBSITE

Username:

Date/Password:

Date/Password:

Date/Password:

Date/Password:

Date/Password:

WEBSITE

Username:

Date/Password:

Date/Password:

Date/Password:

Date/Password:

Date/Password:

WEBSITE

Username:

Date/Password:

Date/Password:

Date/Password:

Date/Password:

Date/Password:

U
V

WEBSITE

Username:

Date/Password:

Date/Password:

Date/Password:

Date/Password:

Date/Password:

WEBSITE

Username:

Date/Password:

Date/Password:

Date/Password:

Date/Password:

Date/Password:

WEBSITE

Username:

Date/Password:

Date/Password:

Date/Password:

Date/Password:

Date/Password:

U
V

WEBSITE

Username:

Date/Password:

Date/Password:

Date/Password:

Date/Password:

Date/Password:

WEBSITE

Username:

Date/Password:

Date/Password:

Date/Password:

Date/Password:

Date/Password:

WEBSITE

Username:

Date/Password:

Date/Password:

Date/Password:

Date/Password:

Date/Password:

WEBSITE

Username:

Date/Password:

Date/Password:

Date/Password:

Date/Password:

Date/Password:

WEBSITE

Username:

Date/Password:

Date/Password:

Date/Password:

Date/Password:

Date/Password:

WEBSITE

Username:

Date/Password:

Date/Password:

Date/Password:

Date/Password:

Date/Password:

U
V

WEBSITE

Username:

Date/Password:

Date/Password:

Date/Password:

Date/Password:

Date/Password:

WEBSITE

Username:

Date/Password:

Date/Password:

Date/Password:

Date/Password:

Date/Password:

WEBSITE

Username:

Date/Password:

Date/Password:

Date/Password:

Date/Password:

Date/Password:

U
V

WEBSITE

Username:

Date/Password:

Date/Password:

Date/Password:

Date/Password:

Date/Password:

WEBSITE

Username:

Date/Password:

Date/Password:

Date/Password:

Date/Password:

Date/Password:

WEBSITE

Username:

Date/Password:

Date/Password:

Date/Password:

Date/Password:

Date/Password:

U
V

WEBSITE

Username:

Date/Password:

Date/Password:

Date/Password:

Date/Password:

Date/Password:

WEBSITE

Username:

Date/Password:

Date/Password:

Date/Password:

Date/Password:

Date/Password:

WEBSITE

Username:

Date/Password:

Date/Password:

Date/Password:

Date/Password:

Date/Password:

WEBSITE

Username:

Date/Password:

Date/Password:

Date/Password:

Date/Password:

Date/Password:

WEBSITE

Username:

Date/Password:

Date/Password:

Date/Password:

Date/Password:

Date/Password:

WEBSITE

Username:

Date/Password:

Date/Password:

Date/Password:

Date/Password:

Date/Password:

**W
X**

WEBSITE

Username:

Date/Password:

Date/Password:

Date/Password:

Date/Password:

Date/Password:

WEBSITE

Username:

Date/Password:

Date/Password:

Date/Password:

Date/Password:

Date/Password:

WEBSITE

Username:

Date/Password:

Date/Password:

Date/Password:

Date/Password:

Date/Password:

WEBSITE

Username:

Date/Password:

Date/Password:

Date/Password:

Date/Password:

Date/Password:

WEBSITE

Username:

Date/Password:

Date/Password:

Date/Password:

Date/Password:

Date/Password:

WEBSITE

Username:

Date/Password:

Date/Password:

Date/Password:

Date/Password:

Date/Password:

W
X

WEBSITE

Username:

Date/Password:

Date/Password:

Date/Password:

Date/Password:

Date/Password:

WEBSITE

Username:

Date/Password:

Date/Password:

Date/Password:

Date/Password:

Date/Password:

WEBSITE

Username:

Date/Password:

Date/Password:

Date/Password:

Date/Password:

Date/Password:

WEBSITE

Username:

Date/Password:

Date/Password:

Date/Password:

Date/Password:

Date/Password:

WEBSITE

Username:

Date/Password:

Date/Password:

Date/Password:

Date/Password:

Date/Password:

WEBSITE

Username:

Date/Password:

Date/Password:

Date/Password:

Date/Password:

Date/Password:

W
X

WEBSITE

Username:

Date/Password:

Date/Password:

Date/Password:

Date/Password:

Date/Password:

WEBSITE

Username:

Date/Password:

Date/Password:

Date/Password:

Date/Password:

Date/Password:

WEBSITE

Username:

Date/Password:

Date/Password:

Date/Password:

Date/Password:

Date/Password:

WEBSITE

Username:

Date/Password:

Date/Password:

Date/Password:

Date/Password:

Date/Password:

WEBSITE

Username:

Date/Password:

Date/Password:

Date/Password:

Date/Password:

Date/Password:

WEBSITE

Username:

Date/Password:

Date/Password:

Date/Password:

Date/Password:

Date/Password:

WEBSITE

Username:

Date/Password:

Date/Password:

Date/Password:

Date/Password:

Date/Password:

WEBSITE

Username:

Date/Password:

Date/Password:

Date/Password:

Date/Password:

Date/Password:

WEBSITE

Username:

Date/Password:

Date/Password:

Date/Password:

Date/Password:

Date/Password:

WEBSITE

Username:

Date/Password:

Date/Password:

Date/Password:

Date/Password:

Date/Password:

WEBSITE

Username:

Date/Password:

Date/Password:

Date/Password:

Date/Password:

Date/Password:

WEBSITE

Username:

Date/Password:

Date/Password:

Date/Password:

Date/Password:

Date/Password:

WEBSITE

Username:

Date/Password:

Date/Password:

Date/Password:

Date/Password:

Date/Password:

WEBSITE

Username:

Date/Password:

Date/Password:

Date/Password:

Date/Password:

Date/Password:

WEBSITE

Username:

Date/Password:

Date/Password:

Date/Password:

Date/Password:

Date/Password:

WEBSITE

Username:

Date/Password:

Date/Password:

Date/Password:

Date/Password:

Date/Password:

WEBSITE

Username:

Date/Password:

Date/Password:

Date/Password:

Date/Password:

Date/Password:

WEBSITE

Username:

Date/Password:

Date/Password:

Date/Password:

Date/Password:

Date/Password:

WEBSITE

Username:

Date/Password:

Date/Password:

Date/Password:

Date/Password:

Date/Password:

WEBSITE

Username:

Date/Password:

Date/Password:

Date/Password:

Date/Password:

Date/Password:

WEBSITE

Username:

Date/Password:

Date/Password:

Date/Password:

Date/Password:

Date/Password:

Y
Z

WEBSITE

Username:

Date/Password:

Date/Password:

Date/Password:

Date/Password:

Date/Password:

WEBSITE

Username:

Date/Password:

Date/Password:

Date/Password:

Date/Password:

Date/Password:

WEBSITE

Username:

Date/Password:

Date/Password:

Date/Password:

Date/Password:

Date/Password:

WEBSITE

Username:

Date/Password:

Date/Password:

Date/Password:

Date/Password:

Date/Password:

WEBSITE

Username:

Date/Password:

Date/Password:

Date/Password:

Date/Password:

Date/Password:

WEBSITE

Username:

Date/Password:

Date/Password:

Date/Password:

Date/Password:

Date/Password:

Y
Z

WEBSITE

Username:

Date/Password:

Date/Password:

Date/Password:

Date/Password:

Date/Password:

WEBSITE

Username:

Date/Password:

Date/Password:

Date/Password:

Date/Password:

Date/Password:

WEBSITE

Username:

Date/Password:

Date/Password:

Date/Password:

Date/Password:

Date/Password:

WEBSITE

Username:

Date/Password:

Date/Password:

Date/Password:

Date/Password:

Date/Password:

WEBSITE

Username:

Date/Password:

Date/Password:

Date/Password:

Date/Password:

Date/Password:

WEBSITE

Username:

Date/Password:

Date/Password:

Date/Password:

Date/Password:

Date/Password:

SOFTWARE

License Number:

Purchase Date:

Subscription License Renewal Date:

Monthly Fee:

SOFTWARE

License Number:

Purchase Date:

Subscription License Renewal Date:

Monthly Fee:

SOFTWARE

License Number:

Purchase Date:

Subscription License Renewal Date:

Monthly Fee:

SOFTWARE

License Number:

Purchase Date:

Subscription License Renewal Date:

Monthly Fee:

SOFTWARE

License Number:

Purchase Date:

Subscription License Renewal Date:

Monthly Fee:

SOFTWARE

License Number:

Purchase Date:

Subscription License Renewal Date:

Monthly Fee:

SOFTWARE

License Number:

Purchase Date:

Subscription License Renewal Date:

Monthly Fee:

SOFTWARE

License Number:

Purchase Date:

Subscription License Renewal Date:

Monthly Fee:

SOFTWARE

License Number:

Purchase Date:

Subscription License Renewal Date:

Monthly Fee:

SOFTWARE

License Number:

Purchase Date:

Subscription License Renewal Date:

Monthly Fee:

SOFTWARE

License Number:

Purchase Date:

Subscription License Renewal Date:

Monthly Fee:

SOFTWARE

License Number:

Purchase Date:

Subscription License Renewal Date:

Monthly Fee:

SOFTWARE

License Number:

Purchase Date:

Subscription License Renewal Date:

Monthly Fee:

SOFTWARE

License Number:

Purchase Date:

Subscription License Renewal Date:

Monthly Fee:

SOFTWARE

License Number:

Purchase Date:

Subscription License Renewal Date:

Monthly Fee:

SOFTWARE

License Number:

Purchase Date:

Subscription License Renewal Date:

Monthly Fee:

SOFTWARE

License Number:

Purchase Date:

Subscription License Renewal Date:

Monthly Fee:

SOFTWARE

License Number:

Purchase Date:

Subscription License Renewal Date:

Monthly Fee:

SOFTWARE

License Number:

Purchase Date:

Subscription License Renewal Date:

Monthly Fee:

SOFTWARE

License Number:

Purchase Date:

Subscription License Renewal Date:

Monthly Fee:

SOFTWARE

License Number:

Purchase Date:

Subscription License Renewal Date:

Monthly Fee:

SOFTWARE

License Number:

Purchase Date:

Subscription License Renewal Date:

Monthly Fee:

SOFTWARE

License Number:

Purchase Date:

Subscription License Renewal Date:

Monthly Fee:

SOFTWARE

License Number:

Purchase Date:

Subscription License Renewal Date:

Monthly Fee:

BROADBAND MODEM

Model:

Serial Nbr:

Mac Address:

Administration URL/IP Address:

WAN IP Address:

Username:

Date/Password:

Date/Password:

Date/Password:

Date/Password:

ROUTER/WIRELESS ACCESS POINT

Model:

Serial Nbr:

Factory Default Admin IP Address:

Factory Default Username:

Factory Default Password:

User Defined Admin URL/IP Address:

User Defined Username:

User Defined Password/Date:

BROADBAND MODEM

Model:

Serial Nbr:

Mac Address:

Administration URL/IP Address:

WAN IP Address:

Username:

Date/Password:

Date/Password:

Date/Password:

Date/Password:

ROUTER/WIRELESS ACCESS POINT

Model:

Serial Nbr:

Factory Default Admin IP Address:

Factory Default Username:

Factory Default Password:

User Defined Admin URL/IP Address:

User Defined Username:

User Defined Password/Date:

BROADBAND MODEM

Model:

Serial Nbr:

Mac Address:

Administration URL/IP Address:

WAN IP Address:

Username:

Date/Password:

Date/Password:

Date/Password:

Date/Password:

ROUTER/WIRELESS ACCESS POINT

Model:

Serial Nbr:

Factory Default Admin IP Address:

Factory Default Username:

Factory Default Password:

User Defined Admin URL/IP Address:

User Defined Username:

User Defined Password/Date:

WAN SETTINGS

MAC Address (see Broadband Modem):

IP Address (see Broadband Modem):

Host Name (if required by ISP):

Domain Name (if required by ISP):

Subnet Mask:

Default Gateway:

DNS—Primary:

DNS—Secondary:

LAN SETTINGS

IP Address:

Subnet Mask:

DHCP Range (if DHCP enabled):

WIRELESS SETTINGS

SSID (Wireless Network Name):

Channel:

Security Mode:

Shared Key (for WPA):

Passphrase (for WEP):

WAN SETTINGS

MAC Address (see Broadband Modem):

IP Address (see Broadband Modem):

Host Name (if required by ISP):

Domain Name (if required by ISP):

Subnet Mask:

Default Gateway:

DNS—Primary:

DNS—Secondary:

LAN SETTINGS

IP Address:

Subnet Mask:

DHCP Range (if DHCP enabled):

WIRELESS SETTINGS

SSID (Wireless Network Name):

Channel:

Security Mode:

Shared Key (for WPA):

Passphrase (for WEP):

WAN SETTINGS

MAC Address (see Broadband Modem):

IP Address (see Broadband Modem):

Host Name (if required by ISP):

Domain Name (if required by ISP):

Subnet Mask:

Default Gateway:

DNS—Primary:

DNS—Secondary:

LAN SETTINGS

IP Address:

Subnet Mask:

DHCP Range (if DHCP enabled):

WIRELESS SETTINGS

SSID (Wireless Network Name):

Channel:

Security Mode:

Shared Key (for WPA):

Passphrase (for WEP):

NOTES

NOTES

NOTES

NOTES